invert

Secret Power

to Joy, Becoming a Star, and Great Hair Days

A personal Bible study on the book of Philippians

Susie Shellenberger

ZONDERVAN™

GRAND RAPIDS, MICHIGAN 49530 USA

Dedicated to

Lawana Isaacs Shellenberger.

Thank you for the joy and
completion you bring to
our family.

Table of Contents

Introduction

READ THIS FIRST!

Ugh! Carrie groaned as she rolled over and switched off the lamp next to her bed. *I'm so frustrated. I've been a Christian for almost an entire year, and it feels like I'm still struggling with the same ol' things every single day.*

She closed her eyes and listened to the crickets outside her window while her thoughts continued to bounce off the walls of her mind. *Ashleigh's always talking about what God is teaching her. It seems as though she always has something positive to share at youth group. Why can't I grow spiritually like that?*

Carrie turned over on her side and opened one eye in time to watch her cat stretch by the foot of her bed. *I just don't seem to grow at all spiritually,* she thought. *I wonder what's wrong? I go to church, I'm involved in youth group, and I enjoy Sunday school. What gives?*

Her cat purred his satisfaction when Carrie reached down and brought him to her side. She stroked his neck and scratched behind his ears.

I love God, she thought. *And I really want to be a strong Christian. I guess I just don't know how.* Frustrated, she turned over again and finally fell asleep with the cat next to her feet.

Carrie was missing one ingredient in the recipe for a spiritually victorious life: She wasn't studying the Bible!

MAJORLY IMPORTANT

Check out what the apostle Paul has to say about the importance of the Bible in our lives: "The whole Bible was given to us by inspiration from God and is useful to teach us what is true and to make us realize what is wrong in our lives; it straightens us out and helps us do what is right. It is God's way of making us well prepared at every point, fully equipped to do good to everyone" (2 Timothy 3:16-17, *The Living Bible).*

Wow! Since the Bible is so important, doesn't it make sense that we should take it seriously? But how can we take it seriously if we don't read it? And if we're not reading it, we can't study it. And if we're not studying it, we're unable to apply it to our lives.

So think of the Bible as God's personal love letter to you. It's his personal way of communicating with you—talking to you, guiding you, and helping you.

ATTENTION!

Calling all Secret Power Girls! If you're not an S.P.G. and want to become one, you're officially invited to read the first Secret Power Girl book ever written: *Secret Power for Girls: Identity, Security, and Self-Respect in Troubling Times.* It will not only explain what an S.P.G. is, but it will also explain how to become one! You can get a copy of this book at www.youthspecialties.com/store.

You really *do* need to read it before you tackle this book. But until you can add it to your personal collection, I'm not going to keep you in suspense. That wouldn't be fair, right?

A Secret Power Girl is someone (just like you!) who is living with a supernatural power—a power greater than Harry Potter has even thought about, and a power beyond adequate description. This mighty power is strong enough to restore sight to a blind person, make deaf people hear, enable lame kids to run, and even raise a dead person back to life! If you haven't already guessed it, this mighty power is the power of the Holy Spirit—God living inside of *you*.

Do you realize what that means? It means the same mighty power that Jesus Christ lived his life with day after day as he walked the dirt roads of the earth, can be *yours* to claim and live your life with day by day as you walk the hallways of your school, interact with your friends, and live with your family members.

Once you've surrendered everything to the lordship of Jesus Christ—

Hey! Wait a second. What's lordship? *And what do you mean when you say* surrender?

Great questions! And that's why you need to read the first book first. It explains all that and a whole lot more. But once you've established a relationship with God through his Son, Jesus—

Sorry, but I gotta interrupt you again. What do you mean relationship with God? *You make it sound like we can actually know God.*

You can! And it's an extremely exciting relationship! And once you *have* that relationship, you grow closer and closer to him—kind of like you would with a best friend—only your relationship with Christ goes much deeper. He becomes your Savior (the only One who can save you from the sin you were born with), your Guide (he'll show you what to do in the tough day-to-day situations you encounter), your Lord (he created you and wants to be in charge of you—not to treat you like a puppet, but to show you how to get the very most out of life), and yes, your very best Friend forever and ever. And as you grow closer to him, and as you continue to surrender every area of your life to him, you learn to live in his power instead of your own. And that's when life REALLY gets exciting! That's what being a Secret Power Girl is all about.

So now do you understand why it's so important to read the first book first?

Yeah. And I promise I'll order it. But meanwhile, I already have this one, so can I go ahead and read it?

Sure. As long as you know that you may not fully understand some of the things we talk about until you—

Read the first book. Okay.

This book is for girls who want to get the most out of their Secret Power living. It's a Bible study.

You mean I gotta read the whole Bible with this book?

No. (Though I hope you'll eventually read the whole Bible. It's truly fascinating!) In this book, we're just focusing on one small part of the Bible. Just one book. It's the book of Philippians.

I'm not even sure anyone in my family has a Bible! Does that mean I can't read this book?

Tell you what. I'll include the book of Philippians inside this book in case you don't have a Bible of your own. But I want you to seriously consider getting your own Bible—one you can carry around with you, underline stuff while you're reading, and be proud to own. A special youth Bible would be a great thing to add to your birthday or Christmas list.

And for those of you who already have your own Bible, you'll need it for this book. I'll include specific questions that you'll only be able to answer with your own Bible.

By the way, this Bible study is designed so you can do it alone or with a friend.

So I call my best friend and we can do it together?

Sure! In fact, sometimes a friend can hold you accountable.

Accounta-what-a-ble?

Accountable. It means she can encourage you to read and complete each section, and you can do the same for her. It also means you can discuss what you're reading together and pray for one another.

Cool!

Ready?

Can I grab something to drink before we get started?

Sure! And while you're at it, how about pouring me a glass of lemonade? Go grab your Bible (if you have one) and a pen, and meet me on the next page in five minutes!

Oh! One more thing: I'll break down each chapter of our Bible study into different "bites." You can do the whole thing all at once, or you can complete a different bite each day.

Your Secret Power Sister,

Susie Shellenberger

Having a Bad Day,
but Still Happy!

(Note: Each chapter of this Bible study is divided into bite-size chunks that you can either swallow all at once or spread out and complete over a period of time. Try to complete one entire bite at each sitting, okay?)

Philippians

Where is it? In the New Testament. (Right after Ephesians and right before Colossians.)

Who wrote it? Paul.

Who was he? Paul was an apostle of the Lord Jesus Christ, but he sure took an interesting route to get there! He used to hate Christians. In fact, he even persecuted them. But God temporarily blinded him and helped him see that what he was doing was wrong. When that happened, Paul gave his life to God. You can read the whole story in Acts 9. After Paul began serving God, he wrote several letters (books of the New Testament) to fellow Christians. The book of Philippians is a letter he wrote to the church in the city of Philippi.

BITE #1

[From] Paul and Timothy, servants of Christ Jesus. To all the saints in Christ Jesus at Philippi, together with the overseers and deacons. (Philippians 1:1)

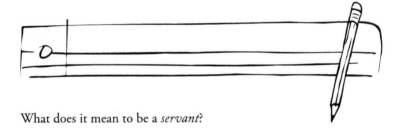

What does it mean to be a *servant?*

Identify a specific time in your life when you served someone. (Maybe your mom was sick and you brought her breakfast in bed; or you put someone else's needs ahead of your own.)

Identify a specific time in your life when someone served *you*.

Paul identifies himself as Jesus Christ's servant. This means...

_____ a. Once he gets to heaven, he has to do chores throughout eternity.

_____ b. He gets a weekly allowance from heaven.

_____ c. He has totally surrendered his life to Jesus and is committed to serving him.

_____ d. He must be pretty good at running the vacuum and emptying the dishwasher.

Guess what! If you chose the third answer, you're on the *right track*. Paul is reminding all of his readers (that's you!) that Jesus Christ is the *Master*. He's the One in charge—not us. *He is Lord*; we are his servants. And we don't serve him out of a grudging "have-to" attitude, but we serve our heavenly Father out of *joy and gratitude* for all he's done for us!

This makes me feel—

_____ a. Like celebrating! After all, Jesus gave his life for me! So the least I can do is serve him with my life.

_____ b. Angry. I don't want to serve anyone.

_____ c. Sleepy. All this talk about servanthood makes me want a nap.

_____ d. Confused. I don't know how to serve God.

The way you can serve God is by giving him your **whole** life. Your **entire** life. Everything in your life. This is called **complete surrender**. And when you do that, you serve Christ by your very lifestyle. And guess what—that brings **true joy**! (More about that later. Let's get back to the Scripture.)

In the first verse of this letter, Paul addresses **all the believers** as *saints*. If you're a believer (a Christian—someone who has asked Christ to forgive her sins and is living in obedience to him), Paul identifies **you** as a saint!

WOW! I—

_____ a. Never thought of myself that way.
_____ b. Realize it's only possible because of Jesus living inside me.
_____ c. Am kind of scared because that's a lot to live up to!
_____ d. Better take this Bible study seriously.

BITE #2

Grace and peace to you from God our Father and the Lord Jesus Christ. (Philippians 1:2)

Have you ever stopped to think about what grace really is? Read the following scenario and try to identify when grace is given.

> *Kaley was walking through the front door of her house when she heard the phone ringing. She tossed her books on the dining room table and rushed to pick up the receiver.*

> *"Kaley? It's Monica. My older sister and I were going to see the early showing of* A Princess Forever *at 4:45. But she's not*

feeling well, and she said you could have her ticket. How 'bout it? Wanna go?"

"I'm dying to see that movie!" Kaley said. "But I have a book report due tomorrow, and I still have five more chapters to read!"

"Free ticket, Kaley! Come on. My mom and I can pick you up in 10 minutes."

"Okay, I'll go."

Monica and Kaley munched on popcorn and drinks during the movie and giggled at the lead character. When Kaley got home, she picked up her book and began reading. She had four chapters left when her brother knocked on her door and told her she had an e-mail waiting for her.

I really shouldn't answer it now, *she thought.* I need to keep reading. But I could answer it quickly and then get back to the book.

So she went downstairs to the family office and absorbed herself in e-mail. An hour later Kaley headed toward her room to finish the book but noticed her parents watching her favorite nighttime drama on television.

"Oh, I forgot that was on tonight!" she said.

"Shouldn't you be reading your book?" her mom asked.

"I'm almost done," Kaley replied. "I'll just watch the rest of this with you guys and finish the book in a few minutes."

By the time the show ended, Kaley could barely keep her eyes open. She struggled to read another chapter in her book and finally fell asleep.

The next morning when Mrs. McCormack asked Kaley for her book report, Kaley approached her teacher's desk.

"Mrs. McCormack, I'm almost finished with the book. I have two chapters left. Is there any way I can turn it in tomorrow?"

"Kaley, you've known about this assignment for three weeks!"

"I know. I'm sorry."

"Is there a reason you need more time? Were you sick? Was there a family emergency?"

"No," Kaley said quietly as she dropped her head. "I really don't have an excuse. I'm just being honest with you. I watched a movie yesterday afternoon when I should have been reading. And when I got home, I stayed up too late watching TV. I don't deserve another chance; I'm just asking for one."

"You're right, Kaley," Mrs. McCormack said. "You really don't deserve another chance. Other students managed to get their reports in on time. But Kaley, I care about you. I believe in you. I think with a little extra time, you'll do a great job on your report. So I'm giving you another chance. You may turn in your report first thing tomorrow morning."

"Oh, thank you, Mrs. McCormack!" Kaley said. "I'll give it my best. You'll love it!"

Mrs. McCormack gave Kaley—

———— A. DETENTION.
———— b. Extra homework.
———— c. A note to take home to her parents.
———— d. Grace.

Kaley experienced grace. She deserved to fail the assignment. But she didn't get what she deserved; she got grace. Guess what! That's the definition of grace: *Not getting what you deserve.*

Because we're all sinners and we have all disobeyed God, we deserve the punishment for sin—death. But when we ask God to forgive us, he gives us grace. In other words, he chooses NOT to give us what we actually deserve (punishment and death), but he forgives us and gives us a brand-new start instead.

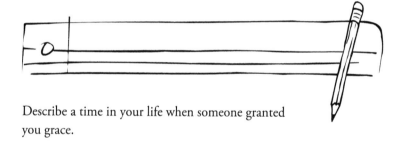

Describe a time in your life when someone granted you grace.

Have you granted someone else grace? If so, describe the situation in the space provided. If you haven't granted grace to others, pray about doing so.

 # BITE #3

I thank my God every time I remember you. In all my prayers for all of you, I always pray with joy because of your partnership in the gospel from the first day until now, being confident of this, that he who began a good work in you will carry it on to completion until the day of Christ Jesus. (Philippians 1:3-6)

How are you being a "partner in the gospel"?

Paul wanted to **thank the Christians** in the church at Philippi for showing him such kindness while he was **in jail** for spreading the gospel. Though they were **separated** by many miles, they were still partners in sharing the Good News of Jesus Christ.

Your church may support **missionaries in Africa** who are sharing Christ with those who haven't yet heard the gospel. Though you can't be in Africa with them, you *can* **partner** with them by—

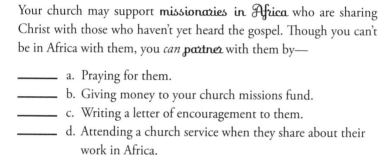

a. Praying for them.

b. Giving money to your church missions fund.

c. Writing a letter of encouragement to them.

d. Attending a church service when they share about their work in Africa.

You can partner with **missionaries around the world** by doing all of the above, but what will help the most is your prayer life. Write out a prayer in the space provided asking God to **strengthen and comfort** those in other countries who are working hard to share his love.

Paul reminds us that God **will** finish the **good work** he started in us. The good work he started in you is: (1) forgiving you of your sins, (2) giving you a desire to follow him, and (3) helping you become more like him.

When you first accepted Christ as your **personal Savior**, you were a baby Christian. But God won't leave you hanging. He'll stay with you! **He'll continue to walk with you** and teach you how to grow stronger in him. **He's committed** to finishing all that he started within you! And he'll keep right on working inside you until you reach heaven.

This makes me feel—

_____ a. Like shouting, "WOW! What an incredible promise!"
_____ b. Like I *will* make it!
_____ c. Like giving God a big hug.
_____ d. Like grinning from ear to ear.

BITE #4

It is right for me to feel this way about all of you, since I have you in my heart; for whether I am in chains or defending and confirming the gospel, all of you share in God's grace with me. God can testify how I long for all of you with the affection of Christ Jesus. (Philippians 1:7-8)

According to the above verse, how should you feel toward other Christians who are involved in spreading the gospel?

And this is my prayer: that your love may abound more and more in knowledge and depth of insight, so that you may be able to discern what is best and may be pure and blameless until the day of Christ, filled with the fruit of righteousness that comes through Jesus Christ—to the glory and praise of God. (Philippians 1:9-11)

When it comes to loving those around me—

———— a. I need help.
———— b. I do really well.
———— c. I get easily annoyed with people who don't agree with me.
———— d. I ask God to help me, and he does.

Have you ever **found yourself** in a situation where you didn't know what to do? Paul tells us that we can "discern what is best." That means **we can know** what's right. According to the above verses, how can you discern what's best?

BITE #5

According to Philippians 1:11, how can we bring glory and praise to God?

———— a. By singing about God.
———— b. Through our honesty.
———— c. By cheering for God.
———— d. By living a life of righteousness.

Now I want you to know, brothers, that what has happened to me has really served to advance the gospel. As a result, it has become clear throughout the whole palace guard and to everyone else that I am in chains for Christ. Because of my chains, most of the brothers in the Lord have been encouraged to speak the word of God more courageously and fearlessly. (Philippians 1:12-14)

Paul is writing these words *from prison.* Imagine you're in jail for talking about God. Paraphrase the above verse (rewrite it in your own words). As you're writing, *pretend* you can smell the dampness and *feel the cold* of the dungeon *jail cell* in which you're held prisoner.

It is true that some preach Christ out of envy and rivalry, but others out of goodwill. The latter do so in love, knowing that I am put here for the defense of the gospel. The former preach Christ out of selfish ambition, not sincerely, supposing that they can stir up trouble for me while I am in chains. (Philippians 1:15-17)

Have you ever had someone **take advantage** of your bad situation? It feels **yucky**, doesn't it? But Paul was **determined** not to get discouraged. Even though he was **imprisoned** for telling others about God, he was able to see **good things** happening in spite of his bad situation. He noticed that others continued to share the Good News. (Some didn't do it for the right reasons, but **he rejoiced** that God's Word was being spread.)

Identify a time in your life when you were able to see something good come out of a difficult situation.

But what does it matter? The important thing is that in every way, whether from false motives or true, Christ is preached. And because of this I rejoice. Yes, and I will continue to rejoice. (Philippians 1:18-19a)

While Paul didn't like being in prison, he maintained a **positive attitude.** It would have been much easier to **give up**, complain, or develop a negative spirit. But Paul **remained joyful** in spite of his circumstances. How do **you** react when things don't go your way?

_____ a. I pout.
_____ b. I get angry.
_____ c. I question God.
_____ d. I try to be positive.

Perhaps you've heard the phrase, "When life gives you lemons, make lemonade." That's basically what Paul was doing. He was making something good out of a difficult situation.

Now it's your turn! Pretend you're running a bumper-sticker factory (do it with a friend, if you can). Create as many bumper-sticker slogans as you can that mean the same thing as the above phrase.

```






```

```






```

```






```

For I know that through your prayers and the help given by the Spirit of Jesus Christ, what has happened to me will turn out for my deliverance. (Philippians 1:19)

Paul doesn't know the future (none of us do!), but he has faith that what happens in the days ahead will be for his good.

What is faith? (It's time to use your own Bible now.) Take a peek at Hebrews 11:1 and write your answer below.

Faith is...

BITE #6

I eagerly expect and hope that I will in no way be ashamed, but will have sufficient courage so that now as always Christ will be exalted in my body, whether by life or by death. (Philippians 1:20)

Paul was extremely focused on bringing glory to God—exalting him. What does it mean to exalt or glorify God?

_____ a. Reflect him.

_____ b. Praise him.

_____ c. Honor him.

_____ d. Proclaim him.

Paul actually did all of the above, and you can too, when you **make it a priority** to exalt the name of Jesus. This is **the perfect remedy** for self-centeredness! By honoring, proclaiming, praising, and reflecting him, you immediately take the attention off yourself and place it on **Christ**.

For to me, to live is Christ and to die is gain. If I am to go on living in the body, this will mean fruitful labor for me. Yet what shall I choose? I do not know! I am torn between the two: I desire to depart and be with Christ, which is better by far; but it is more necessary for you that I remain in the body. Convinced of this, I know that I will remain, and I will continue with all of you for your progress and joy in the faith, so that through my being with you again your joy in Christ Jesus will overflow on account of me. (Philippians 1:21-26)

Paul's **top priority** in life was to proclaim Christ—to speak out boldly for him—and **to bring him honor**. Because Paul was **intently focused** on that one priority, he could honestly say that dying would be greater than living because he'd get to be with Jesus **face to face**.

If you haven't found something (or Someone) worth dying for, **you're not really living**. Think about it: You're not ready to live until you're ready to die.

What are your top priorities? List the four main areas on which you focus your attention.

1.

2.

3.

4.

If Christ isn't in the number one spot in your life, stop right now and ask him to help you rearrange your priorities until he is the most important thing in your life.

 # BITE #7

Whatever happens, conduct yourselves in a manner worthy of the gospel of Christ. (Philippians 1:27a)

"Whatever happens" can include almost anything and everything, can't it? Place yourself in each of the following situations and jot down how you could "conduct yourself in a manner worthy of the gospel of Christ" in each one.

✳ You've noticed that Jessica never has a sack lunch and she never buys a meal ticket for school lunches. She usually sits alone and stares at the floor. What could you do to honor Christ?

✳   Your mom has the flu, and your dad has just come home from work. She's too sick to get out of bed, and your dad is asking if there's anything to eat. You could—

_____ a. Offer to make something (even a peanut butter sandwich would be better than nothing).

_____ b. Beg Dad to order a pizza.

_____ c. Plead with Mom to get up just long enough to get supper together.

_____ d. Sarcastically say, "It's not my fault!"

✳ It took you almost an hour to finish your math homework last night. When you get to school, Julie begs you to let her copy your homework. You don't want to be rude, but you know cheating is wrong. Write out a response that will bring glory to Christ.

✳ Mallory just moved to your area and rode the bus to school for the first time. You overheard other kids from her bus talking about how weird she dresses. You realize that style and fashion differ from state to state, and you want to help her feel as though she has a friend. How can you reach out to Mallory even though everyone else is making fun of her?

BITE #8

Then whether I come and see you or only hear about you in my absence, I will know that you stand firm in one spirit, contending as one man for the faith of the gospel without being frightened in any way by those who oppose you. This is a sign to them that they will be destroyed, but that you will be saved—and that by God. (Philippians 1:27-28)

Paul was *hoping* that whether or not he saw the Christians in Philippi *in person* or just heard about them through others, he would hear of the *good reputation* they had. What's a reputation?

_____ a. It's what other people think about you.
_____ b. It's a label you can sew in the back of your clothes.
_____ c. It's something you use to get your laundry really clean.
_____ d. It's something you can purchase off eBay.

Hey, I hope you chose the first answer! *God wants you to develop a reputation.* He wants others to respect you because of the way you live. What kind of reputation does he want to help you develop? (Circle all that apply.)

Paul also tells the Christians in Philippi that he hopes they'll "stand firm in one spirit." What does it mean to be "in one spirit"?

———— a. It means I always have to agree with everyone around me.

———— b. It means we all dress alike.

———— c. It means we can agree to disagree as long as we're still united.

———— d. It means we all have the same name.

Being "in one spirit" doesn't mean you have to think, dress, or talk alike. But it *does* mean you'll strive to live in harmony. In other words, when someone tries to pick a fight with you, you won't go there. And when someone starts an argument, you'll quickly dissolve it. You'll be united in purpose and goals.

What about your youth group? Is it united? Or is it full of cliques? What specifically can you do to encourage the teens in your group to be "in one spirit"?

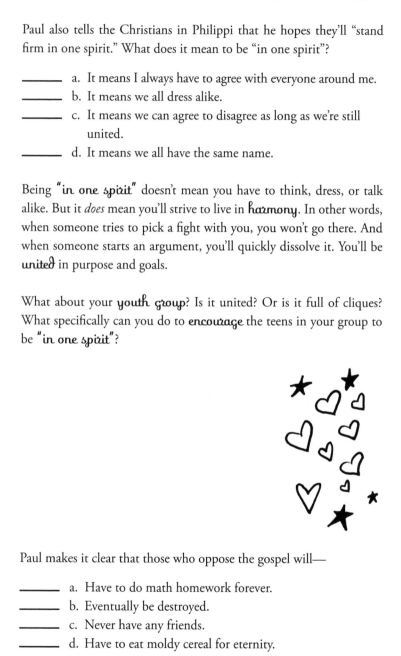

Paul makes it clear that those who oppose the gospel will—

———— a. Have to do math homework forever.

———— b. Eventually be destroyed.

———— c. Never have any friends.

———— d. Have to eat moldy cereal for eternity.

If you're not *for* Christ, you're *against* him. Paul encourages you **not to be afraid** of those who are against the gospel. Describe a time when someone made fun of you for your faith. How did this make you feel?

BITE #9

When you realize that you know the *King of Kings* on a first-name basis, you have no reason to fear those who don't support your faith. After all, this earth is not your home! Your *real* home—your *eternal* home—*is in heaven* with Christ.

For it has been granted to you on behalf of Christ not only to believe on him, but also to suffer for him, since you are going through the same struggle you saw I had, and now hear that I still have. (Philippians 1:29-30)

Paul was **imprisoned** for sharing his faith. Today there are Christians around the world who are also being **persecuted** for their faith. Some are tortured, sold as slaves, or even killed. If you're a Christian, you can expect to be made fun of (at some point in your life) because of your **faith in God**. Your persecution may not be as severe as Paul's, but it will be **real** and it will **hurt**. How will you react the next time someone disses you because of your relationship with Christ?

BITE #10

GRAB A FRIEND

You did it! You made it all the way through the first chapter of Philippians. You're a Secret Power Girl who is growing closer to Christ because you're taking his Word seriously.

Now grab a friend and discuss the following questions together.

✱ Paul labeled himself as a servant of Christ; therefore he served those around him. In what ways can I serve others to prove my love and service for Christ?

✱ Paul thanked God every time he remembered the Christians in Philippi. Stop right now and thank God for your friendships.

✱ Have I reflected Christ this week? If so, how?

✱ Was there a difficult situation I encountered this week in which I could have done a better job of seeing the good?

MEMORIZE IT!

Try to memorize this verse with your friend and say it to each other the next time you get together:

He who began a good work in you will carry it on to completion until the day of Christ Jesus. (Philippians 1:6)

MY JOURNAL

Okay, S.P.G., this is your space, so take advantage
of it. You can do whatever you want here,
but try to always include the following:

* List your prayer requests. (Later, as God answers them, go back and record the date when he answered your prayer.)

* Copy down any verse we studied in the previous chapter that you don't understand. Then let this be a reminder to ask your parents, Sunday school teacher, pastor, or youth leader about it.

* Jot down what stood out the most from this chapter.

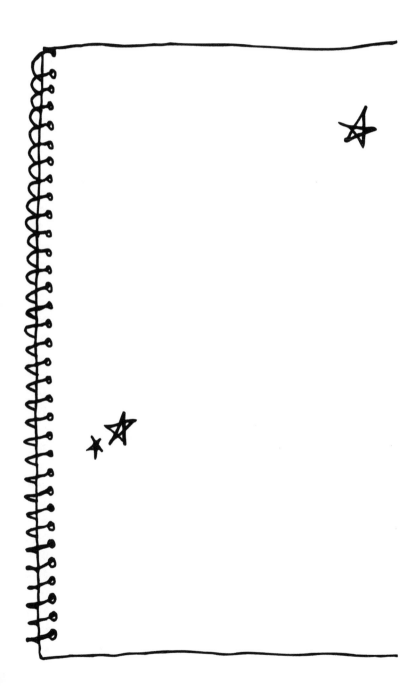

Becoming a STAR!

BITE #1

If you have any encouragement from being united with Christ, if any comfort from his love, if any fellowship with the Spirit, if any tenderness and compassion, then make my joy complete by being like-minded, having the same love, being one in spirit and purpose. (Philippians 2:1-2)

We're reading from the *New International Version* of the Bible, but there are several other versions. You may even own another version. Check out how this second chapter of Philippians begins in *The Living Bible*: "Is there any such thing as Christians cheering each other up?"

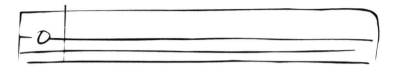

Why is it important that we encourage or "cheer up" one another?

Describe a specific time when you "cheered up" another Christian.

Describe a specific time when a Christian cheered *you* up.

Paul is emphasizing *spiritual unity* among the believers because he knew how fast discord can tear people apart. When you have an argument with teens in your youth group or with family members, how does it make you feel?

_____ a. Yucky.
_____ b. Frightened.
_____ c. Separated.
_____ d. Upset.

You probably feel all of the above! And as *God's children,* he wants us to get along. Non-Christians are watching us. If they see peace, *harmony,* love, and *encouragement* among us, they'll want what we have. But if they notice hatred, *anger,* and *fighting,* they won't have anything to do with Christianity. *How you act and react* can have a *huge impact* on those around you.

Describe one situation in the past few days in which you should've acted or reacted more in love instead of the way you did.

BITE #2

Do nothing out of selfish ambition or vain conceit, but in humility consider others better than yourselves. (Philippians 2:3)

Are there some areas in your life in which you struggle with selfishness? Write out a prayer in the space provided, asking God to help you with those specific areas.

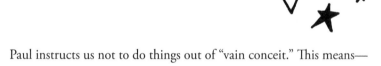

Paul instructs us not to do things out of "vain conceit." This means—

_____ a. Using bad language.
_____ b. Thinking only of myself.
_____ c. Watching TV all the time.
_____ d. Being constantly angry.

When someone is **vain** or **conceited**, she has an excessively high and unrealistic opinion of herself. **Everything centers around her,** and she puts her own needs and wants in front of others'. This is exactly the **opposite** of how Christ wants us to live! Paul reminds us that God desires us to live in humility—thinking of others as better than ourselves. When we **learn to develop** this kind of thinking, it automatically helps us keep a **right attitude.**

Check out the following scenarios and decide if they reflect a humble attitude or a conceited attitude. Circle the correct answer.

✳ Letting your brother have the last helping of mashed potatoes at dinner.

CONCEITED   HUMBLE

✳ Taking cuts in the lunch line at school.

CONCEITED   HUMBLE

✳ Placing your books next to you on the bus so no one else can sit in your row.

CONCEITED   HUMBLE

✳ Running ahead of the others to grab the front seat in your car pool.

CONCEITED   HUMBLE

✳ When Mr. Rhodes commends you for a job well done on your group science project, you quickly mention that Kelly, Amber, and Joey added a lot.

CONCEITED   HUMBLE

✳ There's one front-row seat left at the concert your youth group is attending. Michelle—the new girl—doesn't know anyone. You tell her to take that seat in the front row with the others, while you find a seat farther back.

CONCEITED   HUMBLE

BITE #3

Each of you should look not only to your own interests, but also to the interests of others. (Philippians 2:4)

When someone is self-centered, she—

———— a. Doesn't focus on other people's needs.
———— b. Wears a T-shirt advertising that fact.
———— c. Talks about herself a lot.
———— d. Is horrible at sports.

The **self-centered gal** is constantly thinking and talking about herself, and this prevents her from focusing on other people's needs. Jesus *wants* you to **notice when others are hurting**, lonely, and need encouragement.

What would be different about your life if you really put other people first?

List three things you can do this week to focus on other people's needs. (Example: I can cook dinner for my family.)

1.

2.

3.

Each of you should look not only to your own interests, but also to the interests of others (Philippians 2:4).

Describe how you feel when people put *your* needs and interests ahead of their own.

Why is it important to concentrate on other people's needs and interests?

_____ a. It helps us to become popular.

_____ b. That's what Jesus did and he wants us to do it too.

_____ c. It makes people want to vote for us when we run for class office.

_____ d. By being interested in the needs of others, we can find out how to help them better.

Jesus was constantly thinking about others! Grab your Bible and check out Ephesians 5:1. What specifically are you told to do?

_____ a. Bake bread for your neighbors.

_____ b. Invite people to church.

_____ c. Stay away from bad movies.

_____ d. Imitate God.

When you zero in on other people's interests and needs, **you're doing what Jesus Christ did** when he walked the earth. How can you help others if you don't know what their needs are? If you don't know that Jennifer's dad lost his job and she can't afford to go on the retreat with your youth group, you won't be able to share your baby-sitting money with her. Paul is telling the Christians in Philippi (and us!) that if we're serious about **becoming all God wants us to be**, we'll reach out to others and make a **concentrated effort** to meet their needs.

BITE #4

Your attitude should be the same as that of Christ Jesus: Who, being in very nature God, did not consider equality with God something to be grasped, but made himself nothing, taking the very nature of a servant, being made in human likeness. (Philippians 2:5-7)

If anyone had the right to **pull rank**, be first in line, or demand his own way, **it was Jesus**. After all, he came from the greatest kingdom that exists and willingly chose to live in **our** world and walk **our** dirt roads. He's the King!

But instead of demanding his **rights** or pushing for his **own way**, he became a servant to humanity. *He* served *us*! Check out John 13:4-5. What did Jesus do in this particular situation to serve his disciples?

List eight ways you can be a servant. I'll give you a few suggestions, and you fill in the rest.

1. I can surprise my parents by cleaning the entire house.

2.

3.

4.

5. I can rake the leaves in my neighbor's yard—for free!

6.

7.

8.   I can visit an elderly member of our church who's now a shut-in and can no longer come to services.

And being found in appearance as a man, he humbled himself and became obedient to death—even death on a cross! (Philippians 2:8)

It's easy for us to get caught up with our rights, isn't it? We see television commercials with lawyers telling us how to sue for damage that's been done to us, or for money that's owed to us for being inconvenienced. Maybe you've caught yourself thinking, *Hey, he had no right to say that to me!* Or *That's not fair! I've got my rights!*

It certainly wasn't fair that Jesus was tried as a criminal and crucified. He was completely innocent! Talk about rights. He could have commanded a bazillion angels to rescue him from the cross, but he chose instead to be obedient to the will of the Father. He chose to pay our death penalty for sin so we wouldn't have to!

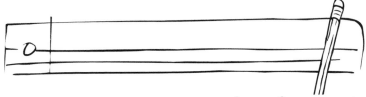

Take a few minutes to write out a prayer of gratitude to Jesus, who didn't demand his royal rights, but instead loves you so much that he took your place on the cross.

BITE #5

Therefore God exalted him to the highest place and gave him the name that is above every name, that at the name of Jesus every knee should bow, in heaven and on earth and under the earth, and every tongue confess that Jesus Christ is Lord, to the glory of God the Father. (Philippians 2:9-11)

What does it mean to be exalted?

_____ a. To use salt on everything you eat.

_____ b. To be lifted higher and honored more than anyone or anything.

_____ c. You're exhausted all the time.

_____ d. You don't have to fight in a war.

Because of Jesus' **total obedience** to his heavenly Father, God chose to honor him by making his name holy, powerful, and always worthy of praise. We often hear the name of Jesus used **sarcastically** on TV shows and in movies. **This deeply grieves God.** Paul reminds us that **there will come a day** when every single person in the entire world will bow in submission to the **authority of Jesus Christ.** Many people use his name carelessly today, but they'll realize their **mistake** as they bow in allegiance to him in the future.

How do *you* use the name of Jesus?

_____ a. Carelessly.

_____ b. Reverently.

_____ c. Sarcastically.

_____ d. I never use it.

Strive to always speak the name of Jesus with **reverence, love,** and **gratitude.** And when you hear his name being used in ways that grieve the heart of God, **stop** and **pray** at that very moment for the person who used Christ's name flippantly.

Therefore, my dear friends, as you have always obeyed—not only in my presence, but now much more in my absence—continue to work out your salvation with fear and trembling, for it is God who works in you to will and to act according to his good purpose. (Philippians 2:12-13)

As Paul begins this Scripture, he alludes to the Christians in Philippi as being people of integrity. What *is* integrity?

_____ a. I think it's a sports car.

_____ b. It means you act with pure motives not only when people are watching, but also when you're alone.

_____ c. Um, I heard it's a new soft drink.

_____ d. It's a spice used in cooking.

Have you ever known someone who's "talked the talk" but hasn't "walked the walk"? In other words, she acts like a Christian on Sundays at church and with the youth group, but when she's at school it's a completely different story? Or she's a good person when her parents are around, but when she's alone she does things her parents wouldn't agree with?

Integrity is acting in purity and honesty not only when everyone is watching but when you're alone as well. It's not only talking about being a Christian, but it's actually living as a Christian would live! (That's what "walking the walk" is all about.)

Paul also tells us to "work out our salvation with fear and trembling." He's *not* saying that if we work hard enough, we can earn salvation. Check out what Paul tells us in Ephesians 2:13: "But now in Christ Jesus you who once were far away have been brought near through the blood of Christ."

It's Christ's blood that saves us—not our good works. None of us could do enough good things to ever deserve salvation. Find out what John (the disciple closest to Jesus) has to say about salvation. (Time to grab your Bible and look up 1 John 5:12.)

In Romans (another book that Paul wrote), he says this about salvation: "This righteousness from God comes through faith in Jesus Christ to all who believe" (Romans 3:22).

It's very clear that our salvation comes from—

_____ a. Attending church regularly.
_____ b. Being involved in a growing youth group.
_____ c. Reading the Bible every day.
_____ d. Faith in Jesus Christ.

BITE #6

For all have sinned and fall short of the glory of God, and are justified freely by his grace through the redemption that came by Christ Jesus. (Romans 3:23-24)

Who has sinned?

_____ a. My history teacher.
_____ b. Eminem.
_____ c. Anyone in jail.
_____ d. Everyone in the whole world.

All of us were born with sin, and the only way we can be forgiven is to repent of our sins (confess or admit that we're sinners and ask Christ to forgive us). Once we do that, he does forgive us, and we begin living for him. But we continue to "work out our salvation." Not in the sense that we're working to earn it, but we continue to work things through with our heavenly Father for the rest of our earthly lives.

Paul goes on to remind us that God works in us to help us act in a godly manner. This doesn't make you a puppet; rather the power of God surging through you can enable you to live the holy life he calls you to live.

Do everything without complaining or arguing, so that you may become blameless and pure, children of God without fault in a crooked and depraved generation, in which you shine like stars in the universe as you hold out the word of life—in order that I may boast on the day of Christ that I did not run or labor for nothing. (Philippians 2:14-16)

Wow! Paul challenges us to "do everything without complaining or arguing." What have you complained about in the last 24 hours? (Circle all that apply.)

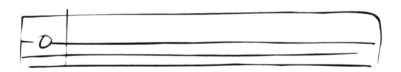

Who was the last person with whom you had an argument? And what did the argument entail?

Looking back on it, was it really necessary to argue about that?

How could you have handled the situation better?

Why is it bad to argue?

_____ a. It makes my face scrunch up in a weird way.
_____ b. If non-Christians see me arguing all the time, it can
           seriously damage my witness.
_____ c. Non-Christians don't want to be around people who say
           they're filled with Christ's love but constantly argue.
_____ d. It can stress out my stomach.

Arguing can actually do all of the above, can't it? No one likes being around someone who complains or argues a lot. We *enjoy* being around those who are positive and show Christ's love.

BITE #7

List your three favorite people to hang out with.

1.

2.

3.

Now list the reason you enjoy being around these people.

1. Because:

2. Because:

3. Because:

Chances are great that you don't enjoy being around these people because they're picking fights or putting you on the defensive. You know **they love you,** and they probably **show it.**

As Christians, Paul encourages us to act in **love, affirmation,** and **encouragement** to each other so non-believers will **see the difference in our lives.** And when they *do* notice the difference, we can tell them **Christ** is the one who's helping us to live a life of love. That's a positive witness!

Paul encourages you to **shine like a star** in this dark world. How can you do that?

To shine like a star, you have to have star qualities. Pause for a second, grab a soda from the fridge, and take this fun star quiz.

_____ True _____ False 1. Stars change over time.

_____ True _____ False 2. Sunlight soaks up the star's energy.

_____ True _____ False 3. Stars that shrink are called white dwarfs.

_____ True _____ False 4. Stars that stop producing light are called black holes.

_____ True _____ False 5. Stars are born when a planet gets too big to contain itself.

ANSWERS

1. True. It may take millions to billions of years for a star to live out its life. Hey, that's a long time! And guess what—eternity is also a loooong time. It's forever! And that's how long your life will last when you belong to Christ. So as you focus on shining like a star, keep the big picture (the eternal one) in focus. When you shine with that in mind, you'll shine much brighter!

2. False. It's the iron that soaks up the star's energy. The iron acts like an energy sponge. This energy is eventually released in a big explosion called a supernova. You are God's star! Strive to absorb all the Spirit into your life so God can create spiritual explosions through you.

3. True. After the nuclear fusion has used up all the fuel it has, gravity will pull the remaining material closer together. The star will shrink. In fact, it may get to be only a few hundred kilometers wide. The star is then called a "white dwarf." It can stay like this for a long time. A Christian, too, can stop shining for God. The Bible tells us to let our light shine. When we stop sharing Christ with those around us, we're hiding our light under a bushel. Ask God to make you keenly aware of how you can more effectively share his light with others.

4. False. When a star stops producing any light at all, it's called a "black dwarf" and it will stay that way forever. When people stop reading the Bible, discontinue praying, and cease to fellowship with other Christians, they stop growing spiritually. They can go from spiritual victory to spiritual defeat in a short amount of time. Don't allow yourself to be spiritually defeated. Cling to God with all of your heart!

5. False. Stars are born in the clouds of dust and gas contained in the galaxy. Doesn't sound very pretty, does it? Spiritual strength is often born from trials and persecution. When things aren't going your way, stop and thank God for the opportunity you have to grow spiritually. Ask God to strengthen your character and your faith. It's during these times that your spiritual light will shine brighter than ever!

Soooo...how's your star quality? Check all that apply.

_____ a. I have to admit that I don't shine very brightly when I'm going through tough times.

_____ b. I'm growing spiritually and in the process of becoming all that God wants me to be.

_____ c. I'm not really growing spiritually right now. But I want to. And that's one reason I'm reading this book. I want to understand the Bible better and learn how to apply it to my life.

_____ d. I'm trying to see the bigger picture of my life. I'm trying to focus on eternal things instead of temporary stuff like, "How can I get him to like me?", "Will I get invited to her party?", and "If only I could get those GAP™ jeans!"

_____ e. I admit I'm not focused on eternal things right now, but I want to be.

_____ f. I'm struggling to be consistent in spending quality time with God.

_____ g. I'm a spiritual sponge. I spend time with God daily, I'm reading my Bible, and I'm plugged into a church.

BITE #8

Go back and reread Philippians 2:15-16. What specifically are you challenged to do as you shine like a star?

What's the "word of life"?

_____ a. A just-released CD by a brand-new pop group.
_____ b. The Bible.
_____ c. A new computer program.
_____ d. God's message of salvation.

If you chose the second and last answers, **you're totally on track with Paul's challenge.** Now the question is—are you doing it? Are you sharing God's message? Are you telling others about Jesus?

_____ a. I invite people to church sometimes.
_____ b. Once in a while I carry my Bible to school.
_____ c. When people ask me about my beliefs, I gladly share my faith with them.
_____ d. I want to talk about my faith, but I'm nervous.

But even if I am being poured out like a drink offering on the sacrifice and service coming from your faith, I am glad and rejoice with all of you. So you too should be glad and rejoice with me. (Philippians 2:17-18)

Paul is saying that **even if he were to die,** he'd die a happy man knowing that he'd helped the Christians in the church at Philippi grow **stronger** in their faith. We tend to think that **sacrifice** is painful. But when you're living your life **100 percent for Jesus**, sacrifice is actually **rewarding**! List some things that Christ sacrificed for you.

I hope in the Lord Jesus to send Timothy to you soon, that I also may be cheered when I receive news about you. I have no one else like him, who takes a genuine interest in your welfare. For everyone looks out for his own interests, not those of Jesus Christ. But you know that Timothy has proved himself, because as a son with his father he has served with me in the work of the gospel. I hope, therefore, to send him as soon as I see how things go with me. And I am confident in the Lord that I myself will come soon. (Philippians 2:19-24)

Paul was serving **jail time** in Rome when he wrote this letter to the Philippians. Even though Timothy was much **younger** than Paul, he was an **encouragement** to the apostle during this time. He visited Paul faithfully and **prayed for him** often.

Even though you're young, you can encourage others who are older than you. List five people who are older than you whom you can encourage.

1.

2.

3.

4.

5.

 # BITE #9

Perhaps you've heard the saying, "Jesus first, Others second, Yourself last equals true JOY." Timothy lived this kind of life. He, like Paul, was genuinely concerned about the spiritual welfare of the Christians in Philippi. They'd both learned to put their own needs aside to focus on how they could help others.

Have you learned the secret of true JOY? Are you making it a practice to keep Jesus first in your life, others second, and yourself last?

_____   a. I want to think of others before myself, but I usually don't.
_____   b. Jesus is absolutely of utmost importance in my life.
_____   c. I enjoy trying to help others and usually put my own needs on the back burner to focus on what someone else needs.
_____   d. I want to develop this kind of genuine joy, but I'll need to totally rearrange my entire life to do so.

But I think it is necessary to send back to you Epaphroditus, my brother, fellow worker and fellow soldier, who is also your messenger, whom you sent to take care of my needs. For he longs for all of you and is distressed because you heard he was ill. Indeed he was ill, and almost died. But God had mercy on him, and not on him only but also on me, to spare me sorrow upon sorrow. Therefore I am all the more eager to send him, so that when you see him again you may be glad and I may have less anxiety. Welcome him in the Lord with great joy, and honor men like him, because he almost died for the work of Christ, risking his life to make up for the help you could not give me. (Philippians 2:25-30)

The church in Philippi had given money to Epaphroditus to deliver to Paul as a gift. While Epaphroditus was with Paul, he became very sick. When he was well enough to travel home, he returned to the Christians in Philippi and gave them this letter from Paul (the book of Philippians) as a thank-you note.

Have you ever written a thank-you note? Sometimes people write thank-you notes after they've received a Christmas or birthday gift. But think about this: The greatest gift ever given to you was given by Jesus Christ. Have you ever thanked him for the gift of eternal life he's given to you? Have you told him how grateful you are for his death on the cross? Take time to write Christ a thank-you note right now.

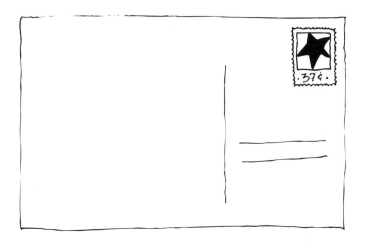

BITE #10

GRAB A FRIEND

You did it! You just completed the second chapter of Philippians. You're a Secret Power Girl who's learning how to apply God's Word to your life! Now grab a friend and discuss the following questions together.

✳ Was there a time this week when I didn't experience true JOY because I failed to put Jesus first, others second, and myself last?

✳ Was there a time this week when I did experience true JOY by putting Jesus first, others second, and myself last?

✳ What specific differences has the "word of life" (verse 16) made in my daily routine this past week?

✳ Paul said he'd find joy even in sacrifice. If his life were poured out like a drink, he'd still be happy because he had helped the Philippians grow stronger in Christ. What sacrifices did I make this week to help someone else grow closer to God?

✳ What sacrifices could I have made this week to help someone else deepen his or her relationship with Jesus?

MEMORIZE IT!

Try to memorize this verse with your friend and say it to each other the next time you get together:

Do everything without complaining or arguing, so that you may become blameless and pure, children of God without fault in a crooked and depraved generation, in which you shine like stars in the universe as you hold out the word of life. (Philippians 2:14-16)

MY JOURNAL

 Okay, S. P. G., this is your space, so take advantage of it. You can do whatever you want here, but try to always include the following:

✳ List your prayer requests. (Later, as God answers them, go back and record the date when he answered your prayer.)

✳ Copy down any verse we studied in the previous chapter that you don't understand. Then let this be a reminder to ask your parents, Sunday school teacher, pastor, or youth leader about it.

✳ Jot down what stood out the most from this chapter.

It's Okay to be a Copycat
(If You're Copying the Right One)

BITE #1

Finally, my brothers, rejoice in the Lord! It is no trouble for me to write the same things to you again, and it is a safeguard for you. (Philippians 3:1)

Think back to your grade school days. You probably learned addition and multiplication by a series of *repetitive lessons* from your teacher. You memorized over and over that two plus two is four. Three plus one is four. Seven times eight equals 56. Eight times seven equals 56. Some things in life simply have to be *learned by repetition.* Paul is repeating something in this third chapter of Philippians that he's already mentioned before. He wants his friends to learn through repetition and through life experience that they can be *joyful.*

Paul never got tired of reminding his Philippian friends to find the positive side of life and focus intently on that. When we choose to zero in on the good things happening around us instead of the bad stuff, it's much easier to keep a good attitude.

Take a moment to think of something less-than-perfect that happened to you in the past few days. Even though your situation wasn't entirely a good one, focus right now on something positive about that situation. Identify it in the space below.

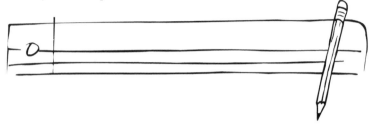

If you had intently searched to discover the positive side of your situation while it was happening, how could that have affected your attitude?

Watch out for those dogs, those men who do evil, those mutilators of the flesh. For it is we who are the circumcision, we who worship by the Spirit of God, who glory in Christ Jesus, and who put no confidence in the flesh. (Philippians 3:2-3)

When Paul mentions dogs, he's actually talking about—

_____ a. Beagles, poodles, and schnauzers.
_____ b. Being kinder to the neighbor's pooch.
_____ c. Bad people.
_____ d. Giant breeds such as Saint Bernards, Great Danes, and
Old English sheepdogs.

Though dogs today are cherished pets, dogs in Paul's time were anything but loved! They roamed the streets, often in packs, and growled at anyone who approached them. They weren't the tame animals we love today. They often **attacked people** who got too close.

Throughout the Bible, **the dog** always stands for the **lowest** thing on the totem pole. When you called someone a dog, you were implying that there could be no one lower. In essence, you were saying that person was the **lowest of the low.**

In this passage, Paul refers to a **group of people** as dogs. They were Judaizers—churchgoers who were messed up in their beliefs. Most of them were full of **spiritual pride.** They thought they were more religious than those around them because they obeyed some very old rules. They taught that it was **necessary** to follow every single one of the Old Testament laws to receive salvation, and they especially focused on circumcision.

While **it's important to follow God's will,** Jesus came to earth and offered his life as a sacrifice so Christians would no longer have to follow all the rules they did before he was born. Until Jesus chose to leave heaven and invade our world with **love** and **forgiveness,** people approached God by sacrifice. That's why the Old Testament is full of stories of believers who sacrificed animals to God for forgiveness. And they couldn't grab just any animal for the job; they had to find a **perfect** one—one **without blemish** or fault. God required the best.

Jesus decided to become the **ultimate sacrifice.** He was perfect. He had **no sin** and **no fault.** So when he died for our sins, people could approach God without searching for a perfect animal offering. **Jesus became our living sacrifice.** He is our perfect offering.

We still need to follow **God's will,** and it's still necessary to live according to the principles in the **Ten Commandments,** but we no longer have to follow all the Old Testament rituals just to **approach God.**

The Judaizers, though, insisted on telling people that they *did* have to continue to follow all these rules. And by telling new Christians this, they were **confusing** folks in the church and causing **trouble.**

Paul wrote to remind the Christians in Philippi that it's not *ever* possible to earn our salvation by following rules. **We become saved through grace!** Salvation is a wonderful **gift** given to us by Jesus Christ when we seek forgiveness for our sins and live in obedience to him.

Have you expressed your thanks today for all God's done for you? Spend some time right now creating a list of things God has done for you. Then pause and say a prayer of thanks.

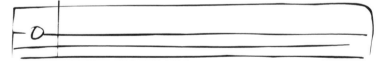

BITE #2

Though I myself have reasons for such confidence. If anyone else thinks he has reasons to put confidence in the flesh, I have more; circumcised on the eighth day, of the people of Israel, of the tribe of Benjamin, a Hebrew of Hebrews; in regard to the law, a Pharisee; as for zeal, persecuting the church; as for legalistic righteousness, faultless. (Philippians 3:4-6)

Though it may sound as if Paul is *bragging* about his accomplishments, he's actually doing *just the opposite*. Yes, he had impressed the Philippians with his credentials, but he was teaching them that no matter how much someone does, *he can never impress God*. (For a *closer peek* at Paul's credentials, check out 2 Corinthians 11 and Galatians 1:13, 24.)

When Paul gave his heart to Jesus, he quickly learned that even the best accomplishments still fall short of God's holiness. If you're depending on your parents' faith to get you into heaven—

_____ a. You're in for a big surprise!
_____ b. You'll have no trouble getting in.
_____ c. You'll bring a smile to God's face.
_____ d. God probably won't even notice.

God *isn't concerned* with heritage, rights, or degrees. None of these things will earn us a *place in heaven* or purchase forgiveness for sins. Again, *salvation is a gift* from God.

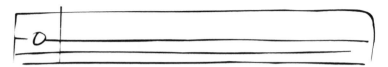

What are some things your friends have done in an attempt to impress you?

How does that make you feel?

What are some ways you've tried to impress God?

How do you think that makes God feel?

Salvation comes through (circle all that apply):

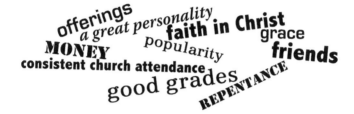

But whatever was to my profit I now consider loss for the sake of Christ. What is more, I consider everything a loss compared to the surpassing greatness of knowing Christ Jesus my Lord, for whose sake I have lost all things. I consider them rubbish, that I may gain Christ and be found in him, not having a righteousness of my own that comes from the law, but that which is through faith in Christ—the righteousness that comes from God and is by faith. (Philippians 3:7-9)

Paul tells his Philippian friends that all his achievements—which he was obsessed with and proud of at one time—now mean *nothing* in light of all that *Christ* has done for him. How can any of us *compare* what we get from God to what little we have to give in return? Can you find a fair trade—something you can offer Jesus in return for his **suffering and death,** God's **forgiveness** of your sins, and your **eternal life**? What could you possibly give to him that would come close to being equal in value to what he's given you? (circle all that apply.)

my bicycle
the ribbons I've earned
my stuffed animal collection
a car
my allowance
a thank you note
a poem
MY PET
my computer
my shoes
the trophies I've won
my favorite christmas gift
A STATE-OF-THE-ART STEREO SYSTEM
my scrapbook

BITE #3

The only thing God desires from you is *you*! How can you give yourself as a gift to God?

———— a. Wrap a ribbon around my head and sit under a
          Christmas tree.
———— b. Earn as much money as I can and give all of it to the church.
———— c. Obey God in all I do.
———— d. Always wear a cross necklace.

I want to know Christ and the power of his resurrection and the fellowship of sharing in his sufferings, becoming like him in his death, and so, somehow, to attain to the resurrection from the dead. (Philippians 3:10-11)

Knowing Christ was the deepest desire of Paul's heart. What are your top five desires in life?

1.

2.

3.

4.

5.

How can we really know Christ? (check all that apply.)

_____ a. Reading the Bible—his letter to us.

_____ b. Searching for him all over the world.

_____ c. Kneeling in a room all by ourselves and waiting for him to speak to us.

_____ d. Plugging into an active, growing church.

_____ e. Traveling to the Holy Land.

_____ f. Talking to him and listening for his voice.

_____ g. Surrounding ourselves with other Christians who know him.

_____ h. Maintaining an active relationship with him.

There are several ways you can get to know Christ better. Think about your best friend. How have you gotten to know her so well?

The *first way* we get to know Christ is by giving our life to him. By trusting him and *spending time with him* (through prayer and reading the Bible), we get to know him better. It also helps to become involved in a church and establish Christian friendships. Paul had done these things and still had a desire to know God more. This teaches us that we can never know God too much. We should always want to know God more and *draw continually closer to him.*

What's the difference between knowing *about* God and truly *knowing* God? Just knowing *about* God doesn't make someone a Christian. Think about it: Even Satan knows about God! It's only when we place our faith in God that we actually begin the process of getting to know him.

BITE #4

Paul has already talked about the importance of Christ, but now he gets a little more specific. He says he wants to know the power of Christ's resurrection. What's he talking about?

_____ a. Paul wants to learn how to raise people from the dead.
_____ b. He wanted to make a movie about seeing dead people.
_____ c. He was power-hungry.
_____ d. Paul wanted to live his life with the same power Christ used to raise himself from the grave.

Let's hike over to another one of Paul's letters for just a second. Check out what he says in Ephesians 3:20 from *The Living Bible*: "Now glory be to God who by his mighty power at work within us is able to do far more than we would ever dare to ask or even dream of—infinitely beyond our highest prayers, desires, thoughts, or hopes."

What does Paul mention in the above verse that he also talks about in Philippians 3:10-11?

_____ a. Power bars.
_____ b. Power.
_____ c. Power walking.
_____ d. Power appetite.

Have you ever really thought about God's power? Think about it right now: The **same mighty power** that raised Jesus from the dead, hung the stars in the sky, made blind people see, and set the entire world in motion *is yours*! That's right. When you invite Christ to take charge of your life, he doesn't just give you a tiny piece of himself. He comes into your life in all his fullness. In other words, you get all of him!

Unfortunately, many Christians simply allow God's power to remain dormant—or stagnant—inside of them. But Paul was saying that he wanted to be the kind of Christian that truly *knew* God's power. He didn't want to simply settle for *having* God's power; he wanted to claim it and live his life in that power.

If you really started to live in Christ's power, what specific things would change in your life?

Paul is saying that to really know the power of the resurrection is to live a power-filled holy life. But he doesn't stop there! He also says he wants to share in Christ's sufferings! Why would he say that?

_____ a. Paul was weird.

_____ b. He watched too much TV.

_____ c. He didn't really know what he was saying.

_____ d. Paul knew that when Christians suffered for their faith,
they grew stronger spiritually.

Are you familiar with Heather Mercer and Dayna Curry? They're two young ladies who were imprisoned by the Taliban in Afghanistan for sharing their faith. When they were finally freed several months later, both said they'd gladly do it all over again for the chance to talk about Christ in that country. The media hailed them as heroes of their faith, but the girls consistently denied that title and said that being jailed drew them closer to Christ.

They wrote a book called *Prisoners of Hope: The Story of Our Captivity and Freedom in Afghanistan* (WaterBrook Press). If you're interested in reading about God working in some truly awesome ways, be sure to check it out. *In the Presence of My Enemies*, by Gracia Burnham and Dean Merrill (Tyndale), is another good book that relates to God's faithfulness through persecution. It's also worth a read.

BITE #5

Okay, it's time to grab your own Bible! Flip to the book of James in the New Testament. Take a peek at James 1:1-18. What does James say will happen to us when we go through difficult times?

Paul knew the **secret** of sharing in Christ's sufferings. Paul had been tortured, shipwrecked, beaten, and harassed. And guess what—he actually **counted it all as a privilege** instead of a hardship. He felt **honored** to suffer for Christ. Instead of focusing on the suffering, Paul focused on **eternity**. He reminded his readers that someday he would share in Christ's resurrection.

The same goes for you! Someday, after all the problems and trials are over, you will get to share in Christ's resurrection too. You can look forward to **eternal life!**

How do *you* typically respond when you're picked on, encounter troubles, or go through a tough time?

Write out a prayer asking God to help you view suffering as a privilege instead of a hardship. Ask God to help you grow closer to him during the tough times and to maintain a positive attitude like Paul did.

BITE #6

Not that I have already obtained all this, or have already been made perfect, but I press on to take hold of that for which Christ Jesus took hold of me. (Philippians 3:12)

Learning to see the good in our suffering is much easier said than done, isn't it? And *Paul admits that.* He lets his friends know that he hasn't totally mastered this goal, but he's certainly *focused on it* and working toward it.

It will probably *take you a while* to master this too. You may not wake up *tomorrow morning* and suddenly see the good side of being made fun of at school. But you can *ask God* to continue teaching you to *see life through his eyes* instead of your own. Eventually, that will make *all the difference!*

Paul says he keeps pressing on. What's he talking about?

———— a. He's really good at ironing.
———— b. He's the one who invented pressing flowers together between the pages of a book.
———— c. His eye is on the eternal prize, and he's not giving up.
———— d. He was under so much pressure that he felt he would soon explode.

When our eyes are fixed on a *specific goal,* it becomes easier to make ourselves continue to the end. Paul had his eyes fixed on Christ and spending eternity with him. Therefore, *even in the midst of his suffering,* he could press onward.

Brothers, I do not consider myself yet to have taken hold of it. But one thing I do: Forgetting what is behind and straining toward what is ahead, I press on toward the goal to win the prize for which God has called me heavenward in Christ Jesus. (Philippians 3:13-14)

Compare what Paul is saying about his Christian life and "straining toward what is ahead" to an athlete running a race. How are the two alike?

We've all made mistakes. There may be some things in your past that you'd like to forget. Unfortunately, many people "live in the past." What does that mean?

_____ a. They live in the same house their entire life.
_____ b. They continue to dwell on the past and allow it to keep them from getting on with life.
_____ c. They stay in second grade forever.
_____ d. They never stop wearing baby clothes.

𝐼t doesn't do any good to dwell on the hurts of the past and allow those hurts to keep us from becoming all God wants us to be. Paul lets his Christian friends know that he's not going to live in the past. He had some big regrets—he formerly persecuted Christians! But he knew God had forgiven him, and he was determined to focus on becoming all that God wanted for the future.

What's something from your past that's holding you back from becoming all God wants you to be?

Will you give that to God right now? Go ahead. Release it. Draw a picture of a grave and bury that stuff from your past inside the grave to symbolize that you're not going to dwell on it any longer.

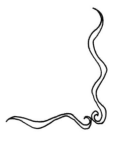

BITE #7

All of us who are mature should take such a view of things. And if on some point you think differently, that too God will make clear to you. Only let us live up to what we have already attained. (Philippians 3:15-16)

Paul reminds us that Christ wants to help us mature in our faith. Spiritual maturity requires *discipline* and *effort*. While Paul realized some will disagree with what he was saying, he was confident that God will eventually show them that growing Christians *shouldn't lower their standards* or become lazy in their spiritual growth. We should all press toward our goal of *becoming Christlike.*

Think back to when you first became a Christian. How have you matured—or grown stronger in your faith since then?

In what areas of your life are you tempted to lower your standards (circle all that apply)?

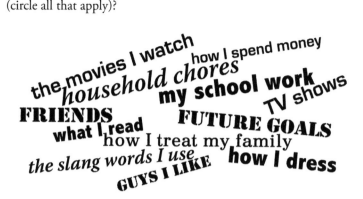

the movies I watch   how I spend money
the household chores   my school work   TV shows
FRIENDS   FUTURE GOALS
what I read   how I treat my family
the slang words I use   GUYS I LIKE   how I dress

How will lowering your standards in the above areas affect your relationship with Christ?

Join with others in following my example, brothers, and take note of those who live according to the pattern we gave you. (Philippians 3:17)

Wow! *Imagine* being so confident in your relationship with Christ— and so *mature in your faith*—that you could easily tell others to *imitate you.* That's what Paul is saying to his friends in Philippi. He wanted them to grow stronger in their faith, so he simply told them to *watch, learn,* and *do as he does.*

How can he do that?

    _____ a. Paul had been in jail too long to know what he was saying.

    _____ b. Paul was intensely focused on imitating Christ, so he could easily tell others to imitate him as he imitated Christ.

    _____ c. Paul knew his friends wouldn't take him seriously, so he was safe in saying that.

    _____ d. Paul was always saying something no one understood.

What's an area of your life in which you could easily tell others to imitate you imitating Jesus?

What's an area of your life in which you'd never tell someone to imitate you?

BITE #8

Let's skip over to another one of Paul's letters for a second. Check out what he says in Ephesians 5:1—"Be imitators of God."

Because Paul was imitating Christ, he could be confident in telling others to imitate him. In essence, he was actually telling them to—

_____ a. Imitate Christ.

_____ b. Mind their own business.

_____ c. Forget about being a copycat.

_____ d. Learn how to cook.

Jesus wants you to imitate him. Remember the phrase, "What would Jesus do?" By asking yourself that question throughout the day, you're teaching yourself to **think about Christ's actions and imitate them.**

So how are you doing? Take this quiz to find out!

1. You just got home from school and your mom asks you to clean the kitchen. You—

_____ a. Throw your backpack on the bed and scream, "I haven't even had a chance to breathe yet!"

_____ b. Watch a little TV first, then start cleaning the kitchen.

_____ c. Suggest that your brother do it instead of you.

_____ d. Begin cleaning the kitchen.

2. Sara doesn't have many friends—probably because she smells bad. You can't figure out if her family doesn't have much money for essentials such as soap and shampoo, or if she just doesn't care. But your friends make fun of her, and she usually sits alone in the cafeteria. You—

_____ a. Place a can of deodorant in her locker with a note that reads, "Get a clue!"

_____ b. Spray a lot of perfume on yourself, then ask her to join you for lunch.

_____ c. Ask your school counselor to talk to her about her hygiene.

_____ d. Smile and ask if you can sit with her.

3. You just purchased some new athletic socks for track, and the total amount comes to $10.50. You hand the clerk $20, and she gives you $10.50 in change. You—

_____ a. Spend the extra money on ice cream.

_____ b. Say, "Don't you know how to count?"

_____ c. Look for her boss and tell him what happened.

_____ d. Smile and return the extra money saying, "You gave me a little too much."

4. You're babysitting and four-year-old Josh wants to play a game of hide-and-seek. But it's time for your favorite TV show. You—

_____ a. Say, "You're such a dork, Josh! Go find a neighbor to play with."

_____ b. Tell him to hide, but sit down and watch your show instead of looking for him.

_____ c. Suggest you play only during commercials.

_____ d. Tickle him and begin the game.

5. Your dad asked you to clean up after the dog in the backyard. You went to Amy's house instead. Later than evening when Dad says, "Did you get everything cleaned up in the backyard?" You say—

_____ a. "Good grief! Do I have to do all the work around here?"
_____ b. "I never wanted that dog anyway!"
_____ c. "Uh, I was gonna do it later."
_____ d. "I'm sorry, Dad. I totally forgot. Amy called, and I ran
           over to her house for a while. I'll do it right now."

It's probably **obvious** what Jesus would do in each situation. But in case you haven't guessed, he'd respond with the last choice in each of the above scenarios. The more you ask yourself, "What would Jesus do?" throughout your day, the more *you'll begin imitating him.*

Take a few minutes to design a "What would Jesus do?" (WWJD?) reminder card right now that you can decorate, paint, or cut in a creative way. Place this card someplace where you'll see it often—on your bedroom mirror, inside your Bible, in your backpack—and every time you see it, *let it serve as a reminder* that God wants to help you learn to imitate him in all you do.

BITE #9

For, as I have often told you before and now say again even with tears, many live as enemies of the cross of Christ. Their destiny is destruction, their god is their stomach, and their glory is in their shame. Their mind is on earthly things. (Philippians 3:18-19)

Just because someone is a member of the church doesn't always mean he or she is living in obedience to Christ. Paul warned his friends that there are some people in the church who are even "**enemies of the cross.**" In other words, they try to fool people into believing they're Christians, but they're not really living as Christ wants them to.

Unfortunately, some people use Christianity as a **crutch.** They say, "Since I'm a Christian, I can do whatever I want to and God will always forgive me." **But this isn't true.** Christianity is an ongoing love relationship with the King of Kings. It's not an excuse to do whatever one wants.

There were clearly people in the church of Philippi who called themselves Christians but didn't live the Christian life. In fact, they tried to **justify** their sinning. This saddened Paul to the point of tears.

Write out a definition for the following terms that describe these certain people Paul talks about—

* Phony

* Hypocrite

* Fake

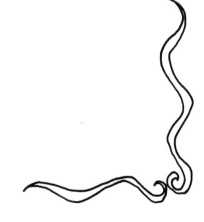

Have you ever pretended to be something or someone you're not?

How did you feel when others found you out?

But our citizenship is in heaven. And we eagerly await a Savior from there, the Lord Jesus Christ, who, by the power that enables him to bring everything under his control, will transform our lowly bodies so that they will be like his glorious body. (Philippians 3:20-21)

As Paul closed this chapter of his letter to his friends in Philippi, he encouraged them to focus on *what really matters* and what is *eternal*—our home in heaven. When you're a *citizen* of a specific country, you get to enjoy the *privileges* of that country. *As Christians, we're citizens of heaven,* and someday we'll get to enjoy all the privileges of heaven—healthy bodies that never get sick, living forever, experiencing no sadness, eternal joy, and so on.

What are you looking forward to experiencing in heaven the most?

BITE #10

GRAB A FRIEND

Congratulations! You just completed the third chapter of Philippians. How does it feel to be a Secret Power Girl who is learning how to apply God's Word to her life? Now grab a friend and discuss the following questions together.

✳ Are there areas of my life in which I tend to lower my standards without realizing it?

✳ What areas of my life prove that I truly *know* Christ?

✳ What evidence of God's power has been demonstrated in my life during the past week?

✳ Paul encouraged his friends to always look for the positive angle in tough situations. Was there a time this week when I should have noticed something positive in a difficult moment, but I failed to do so?

✳ Was there a time this week when I did see the positive side of a difficult situation?

MEMORIZE IT!

Try to memorize this verse with your friend and say it to each other the next time you get together:

But whatever was to my profit I now consider loss for the sake of Christ. (Philippians 3:7)

MY JOURNAL

 Okay, S.P.G., this is your space, so take advantage of it. You can do whatever you want here, but try to always include the following:

✳ List your prayer requests. (Later, as God answers them, go back and record the date when he answered your prayer.)

✳ Copy down any verse we studied in the previous chapter that you don't understand. Then let this be a reminder to ask your parents, Sunday school teacher, pastor, or youth leader about it.

✳ Jot down what stood out the most from this chapter.

Joy^2

BITE #1

Therefore, my brothers, you whom I love and long for, my joy and crown, that is how you should stand firm in the Lord, dear friends! (Philippians 4:1)

Who do you know who consistently "stands firm in the Lord"?

What makes it difficult for you to "stand firm in the Lord"?

I plead with Euodia and I plead with Syntyche to agree with each other in the Lord. (Philippians 4:2)

These two women, Euodia and Syntyche, were members of the church in Philippi and had worked together to help many others come to know Christ and also become involved in their church. They obviously had a **disagreement** over something and weren't getting along.

Paul knew this would have a **negative** effect on those they had won to the Lord, so he urged them to work out their differences and once again **live in harmony.**

How do you usually react to a friend with whom you've had a disagreement (check all that apply)?

_____ a. I try to patch things up right away.

_____ b. I ignore her.

_____ c. I write her a note.

_____ d. I find another friend.

_____ e. I tell others about what she's saying or doing that hurts my feelings.

_____ f. I call her.

_____ g. I pretend nothing happened and continue with our friendship.

_____ i. I pray for her.

_____ j. I talk with my mom or another adult.

It can often be tough to handle a disagreement with a friend, but God wants us to live **without quarreling**. When you're caught in an argument with someone, what kind of impression does that leave with those around you?

What are some common things your youth group tends to quarrel about?

A youth group that's quarreling is ignoring Christ. **No one** can be at peace with God while remaining **bitter** toward someone else. **God is the author of peace.** God wants his children to live and act in **unity**. That doesn't mean we all have to agree with each other. We can have varying opinions but still maintain a harmonious relationship. Oftentimes, we simply have to **agree to disagree.**

BITE #2

Yes, and I ask you, loyal yokefellow, help these women who have contended at my side in the cause of the gospel, along with Clement and the rest of my fellow workers, whose names are in the book of life. (Philippians 4:3)

Paul refers to a "yokefellow." What do you suppose that is?

_____ a. Someone who never eats egg yolks.
_____ b. One who always eats egg yolks.
_____ c. Someone who's allergic to eggs.
_____ d. A partner in the gospel of Christ.

A yokefellow was someone who partnered with another to spread the gospel of Christ. A yokefellow was an intimate friend, a partner in ministry who shared the same godly goals. Can you identify someone like this in your life? Is there someone with whom you can be a yokefellow?

Paul also mentions the "book of life" in this passage. The Bible says this book lists the name of everyone who has accepted Christ as their personal Savior. If you're a Christian, your name is in the book of life!

Imagine that you enter heaven's gates and you're waiting to hear "enter" or "go away." Imagine an angel opening the book of life and scrolling through the pages looking for your name. A smile spreads across the angel's face, and he looks in your eyes and says, "Yes! Here's your name right here!" How would you feel when your name is found?

Now imagine one of your non-Christian friends standing at heaven's gates. The angel searches but never finds your friend's name. How will you feel knowing your friend will be eternally separated from God?

Write down that friend's name and jot down a prayer asking God to help you witness to him or her.

BITE #3

Rejoice in the Lord always. I will say it again: Rejoice!
(Philippians 4:4)

It may seem weird that someone in prison is writing a letter to urge his friends to rejoice. Pretend for a moment that you've been jailed for talking about Christ. Will you try to persuade your friends to feel sorry for you? Will you try to influence your family to find a lawyer? Or will you try to **encourage** your loved ones? Pretending you're in jail right now, write a short letter to your friends and family.

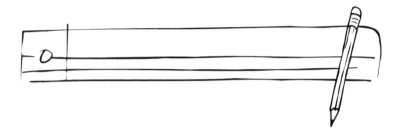

Paul was **so focused on Jesus Christ** that he could **rejoice** no matter what the circumstances. He had a strong, growing relationship with his heavenly **Father.** List three ways your relationship with Jesus affects your life in a powerful way such as this.

1.

2.

3.

Let your gentleness be evident to all. The Lord is near. (Philippians 4:5)

It's time to grab your own Bible! Flip over to the gospel of John and read John 8:1-11. Of what was this woman accused?

_____ a. Stealing.
_____ b. Lying.
_____ c. Murder.
_____ d. Adultery.

The law said she should be killed for the sin she committed. But Jesus chose instead to—

_____ a. Put her in jail.
_____ b. Forgive her.
_____ c. Scold her.
_____ d. Send her to another country.

Jesus acted with **gentleness**. He didn't ignore her sin. He brought it to her attention, dealt with it, **forgave her**, and lovingly sent her on her way.

Imagine you work for a week on a book report. You type it up in a **cool font** on your **computer**, print it out on **colored paper**, and take it to the local copy center to have a **plastic binder** put on it. Your dad, an English professor at the local university, even checked your grammar to make sure **everything is perfect**. You receive an **A** on your report.

You have a really **fun teacher** who sometimes puts wacky stickers on the best papers. So you're not surprised when you receive a funny sticker; after all, you *did* get an **A**!

Sheila sits in front of you, and you notice she **also got a sticker**. But when you strain your eyes to make out her grade, you see she has a **B-**.

Hey, why did Sheila get a fun sticker? you think. *Her paper is hand-written, it's not in a binder, and she didn't get an* A. *What gives?*

What gives is that **your teacher knows more** about Sheila than you do. Mrs. Jenkins knows that Sheila's dad hasn't had a job in eight months, her family is on welfare, and they don't even own a computer. Mrs. Jenkins is aware that Sheila doesn't have a nice desk at home like you do. She had to write her book report while sitting on the floor and using a lamp with a dim light bulb. Sheila doesn't have anyone to correct her grammar, and she doesn't have the money to bind her report. But **she still worked** just as hard as you did, and she **completed** the assignment.

Even though Sheila didn't have a perfect paper—and didn't receive an *A*—Mrs. Jenkins still places great value on Sheila's paper because she knows the story behind it. So she also gave Sheila a cool sticker.

Mrs. Jenkins acted with—

———— a. Ignorance.
———— b. Insanity.
———— c. Jealousy.
———— d. Gentleness.

Gentleness is being able to look **past the situation,** see the reason behind it, and react in kindness. If you were mixing up a batch of gentleness, which ingredients would you need to make it? (Circle all that apply.)

peace   hatred
deceit   jealousy   DISCERNMENT
indifference   bitterness   LOVE
wisdom   CONCERN
fairness   ridicule   softness   suspicion

Identify a time in your life when someone acted in gentleness toward you.

 # BITE #4

Do not be anxious about anything, but in everything, by prayer and petition, with thanksgiving, present your requests to God. (Philippians 4:6)

List the top three things that cause you to worry.

1.

2.

3.

According to the above verse, what does the apostle Paul encourage you to do with your worries (or things that make you anxious)?

_____ a. Write them on a piece of paper and burn them.
_____ b. Give them to God.
_____ c. Cry about them.
_____ d. Run away from them.

If you're constantly anxious (or worrying) about something, what does this have to say about your faith in God to take care of you?

What can we pray about? (Underline everything that's appropriate to take to God in prayer.)

I hope you underlined all of the above because you can actually pray about **everything**! In fact, there's **nothing too small** and there's **nothing too big** for you to take to God in prayer. If you actually prayed about every concern in your life, what kind of difference would that make?

And the peace of God, which transcends all understanding, will guard your hearts and your minds in Christ Jesus. (Philippians 4:7)

Did you catch the promise you have in the above verse? If you do pray about your concerns, God is committed to giving you—

———— a. Peace.

———— b. Straight As.

———— c. Lots of friends.

———— d. More money.

Time to grab your own Bible again. Turn to John 14:27. What kind of peace does John say God wants to give you?

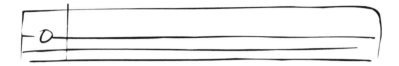

Now read Philippians 4:7 again. What kind of peace does Paul say God wants to give you?

Wow! God's peace sounds incredible, doesn't it? So what's blocking you from experiencing such an amazing peace from your heavenly Father?

BITE #5

Finally, brothers, whatever is true, whatever is noble, whatever is right, whatever is pure, whatever is lovely, whatever is admirable—if anything is excellent or praiseworthy—think about such things. (Philippians 4:8)

Sometimes parents use a particular phrase when they're describing certain TV shows, Internet sites, CDs, or magazines: "Garbage in, garbage out." What do you think that means?

Paul knew that whatever we choose to **focus** on would eventually show up in our **lifestyle.** For example, studies have shown that teens who listen to **violent music,** play **violent games,** watch **violent movies,** and focus consistently on **violence,** eventually **act out violent behavior.** In other words, whatever we put into our mind will eventually come out. It won't stay stuffed down inside us forever.

So Paul **challenges** us to focus on certain kinds of things—good things. Look at the things Paul encourages you to think about, and then list something specific you can focus on that corresponds with each category.

Whatever is RIGHT:

Whatever is PURE:

Whatever is LOVELY:

Whatever is ADMIRABLE:

Whatever is EXCELLENT:

Whatever is PRAISEWORTHY:

One thing that will fit in ALL the categories listed above is—

_____ a. E-mail.
_____ b. Television.
_____ c. The Bible.
_____ d. Microwave popcorn.

Since the Bible is right, pure, lovely, admirable, excellent, and praiseworthy, it makes sense to think about Scripture a lot. How can you do that?

_____ a. By copying a page from the Bible and taping it to my face.
_____ b. By owning six different versions of the Bible.
_____ c. By learning to balance the Bible on top of my head.
_____ d. By memorizing Scripture.

Think about it: The more Scripture you memorize, the more you're filling your life with **truth and purity**. Eventually, that truth and purity will come out. For instance, when you're in a tough situation, God will bring **memorized Scripture** to your mind. And **you'll find wisdom and guidance** in what you've memorized.

At the end of each Bible study chapter, you've been encouraged to memorize a Scripture verse with a friend. How are you doing?

_____ a. I haven't done that yet.
_____ b. I've memorized some of them, but not all of them. (There have only been three so far!)
_____ c. I'm doing it!
_____ d. I'm working on it.

BITE #6

Whatever you have learned or received or heard from me, or seen in me—put it into practice. And the God of peace will be with you. (Philippians 4:9)

It's not good enough to simply *hear, see,* or *know* what God wants us to do; we need to live it! Knowing the right thing doesn't become *active* truth until we *do* it.

Are you *listening* to good sermons, *reading* good devotional books, and *watching* your pastor and youth leader live *good lives?* That's great—but it's *not enough.* You need to actually *live out that truth* and make it a part of your very *lifestyle.*

What's one specific thing you've read about in the Bible, or heard about from your pastor or youth leader, or seen evidenced by other Christians that you can adapt as part of your own *lifestyle?*

I rejoice greatly in the Lord that at last you have renewed your concern for me. Indeed, you have been concerned, but you had no opportunity to show it. (Philippians 4:10)

The best way we can show our love for Christ is reflected in how we treat others. When you're concerned about the well-being of those around you, and when you reach out to help meet their needs, you're actually proving your love for Christ.

Grab your Bible! Check out Matthew 25:31-46. What is the reward for those who feed the hungry and help the poor?

Identify a time in your life when you went out of your way to help someone else.

I am not saying this because I am in need, for I have learned to be content whatever the circumstances. (Philippians 4:11)

Paul knew what it was like to be shipwrecked, lonely, and without the essentials of life. Yet in the midst of all this, he learned to be **content** because true contentment came from his *intimate relationship* with Christ.

We often look to another person to help us feel secure, content, happy, or complete. But true **security**, contentment, happiness, and *wholeness* come only from a strong, growing relationship with God.

Take a peek at the following list and mark each item on a scale from one to 10 (one being the hardest for you to do without, and 10 being the easiest for you to do without).

_____ Soft drinks
_____ My own bed
_____ Toothbrush and toothpaste
_____ Television
_____ Pizza
_____ Computer
_____ Friends
_____ Air conditioning
_____ Parents
_____ Clean clothes

BITE #7

I know what it is to be in need, and I know what it is to have plenty. I have learned the secret of being content in any and every situation, whether well fed or hungry, whether living in plenty or in want. (Philippians 4:12)

Imagine that you don't own a Bible and don't have access to one. How would that affect your relationship with Christ?

How would it affect your attitude? Would you still be able to rejoice?

Paul didn't have a Bible with him, but he *did* have an incredibly strong relationship with God, and that enabled him to rejoice even in the midst of suffering. If you were jailed right now, would your relationship with Christ be strong enough to sustain you?

What can you do to strengthen your relationship with God?

I can do everything through him who gives me strength. (Philippians 4:13)

We often *shy away* from doing things for God because we're *frightened* or don't think we're *talented* enough. Is there something God has been *impressing* on you to do, but you've put it off because you're not confident in this area? Paul realized *there was nothing* he *couldn't* do when God's mighty power *infused his life.* Underline anything from the list below that you've resisted doing due to a lack of confidence, but now realize you *could* do if God so led you.

BITE #8

Yet it was good of you to share in my troubles. Moreover, as you Philippians know, in the early days of your acquaintance with the gospel, when I set out from Macedonia, not one church shared with me in the matter of giving and receiving, except you only; for even when I was in Thessalonica, you sent me aid again and again when I was in need. (Philippians 4:14-16)

The Christians in Philippi had a **history** of showing **kindness** to Paul. This wasn't the first time **he had benefited** from their generosity, and it wasn't the first time he'd had *positive interaction* with them.

Grab your Bible and check out Acts 16:11. Where did Paul sail on his way to Philippi?

_____ a. The Bahamas and the Caribbean.
_____ b. Samothrace and Neapolis.
_____ c. Australia and New Zealand.
_____ d. Tahiti and the Fiji Islands.

Now take a peek at Acts 16:22-38. Whom did Paul lead into a relationship with Jesus Christ in the city of Philippi?

When we **help others** or give a gift of kindness, it not only benefits the receiver, but it also **blesses us as givers**. In fact, the giver is often blessed more than the receiver. **Identify a time** when you gave something to someone and were **truly blessed by the experience.**

Not that I am looking for a gift, but I am looking for what may be credited to your account. I have received full payment and even more; I am amply supplied, now that I have received from Epaphroditus the gifts you sent. They are a fragrant offering, an acceptable sacrifice, pleasing to God. (Philippians 4:17-18)

Paul certainly appreciated the Philippians' gifts to him, but he appreciated their *spirit of generosity and kindness* even more. Flash back to your younger years. Did you ever *make a gift* for your mom or dad? When you gave it to them, they probably received it with much joy, appreciation, and excitement. You felt like the *most important person* in the world, didn't you?

But now that you're older, *you can look back* at that gift and see that it probably wasn't that great. Maybe you colored out of the lines, or the glue hadn't yet dried on your gift, or it even fell apart. But your *parents loved it* because of the *spirit* and *attitude* with which you gave it!

What was the gift and the situation that you're remembering?

BITE #9

And my God will meet all your needs according to his glorious riches in Christ Jesus. (Philippians 4:19)

God is the *giver* of all good things, and he loves to give *good gifts* to his children. He's committed to meeting every single one of your needs, but he may not supply all of them *in this lifetime.* Paul suffered and eventually died; yet he knew in the midst of his pain that any of his needs that weren't met on earth would be met in heaven.

Perhaps you've been praying that a loved one would be healed. God will heal him or her, but he may choose to wait until your loved one is in heaven to bestow complete healing. His timing is not our timing. He's never early, but neither is he ever late. We *can* be assured, however, that God always keeps his word!

The mark of a mature Christian is being able to accept God's ways without understanding them. We won't always understand God's timing, but when we place our ultimate trust in him, we can know beyond doubt that he has our best interests in mind.

What are three things you don't understand and will want to ask God about when you enter heaven?

1.

2.

3.

To our God and Father be glory for ever and ever. Amen. (Philippians 4:20)

What does it mean to give God glory? (Circle all that apply.)

Greet all the saints in Christ Jesus. The brothers who are with me send greetings. All the saints send you greetings, especially those who belong to Caesar's household. (Philippians 4:21-22)

Who are the saints? (Flip back to page 18 if you need a reminder about the saints!)

The grace of the Lord Jesus Christ be with your spirit. Amen. (Philippians 4:23)

Describe how you're currently experiencing the grace of the Lord Jesus Christ.

BITE #10

GRAB A FRIEND

Way to go! You just completed a study of the entire book of Philippians. How does it feel to be a Secret Power Girl who is growing spiritually?

Now grab a friend and discuss the following questions together.

✳ Paul learned to do without many things, and he still experienced true joy. Is there something extra in my life that I could give to someone else and experience the joy of giving?

✳ Paul challenged his friends to think about pure, lovely, and right things. Is there anything in my life that hints that I'm not thinking of positive things (gossip, negative attitude, bad language, and so on)?

✱ Did I use an opportunity this week to share Christ's love with someone who isn't a Christian? If so, describe the situation. Or did I *miss* an opportunity this week to share Christ's love with someone who isn't a Christian? If so, describe the situation.

✱ What specifically can I do to ensure that God's peace guards my mind?

MEMORIZE IT!

Try to memorize this verse with your friend and say it to each other the next time you get together:

Finally, brothers, whatever is true, whatever is noble, whatever is right, whatever is pure, whatever is lovely, whatever is admirable—if anything is excellent or praiseworthy—think about such things. (Philippians 4:8)

MY JOURNAL

Okay, S.P.G., this is your space, so take advantage of it. You can do whatever you want here, but try to always include the following:

∗ List your prayer requests. (Later, as God answers them, go back and record the date when he answered your prayer.)

∗ Copy down any verse we studied in the previous chapter that you don't understand. Then let this be a reminder to ask your parents, Sunday school teacher, pastor, or youth leader about it.

∗ Jot down what stood out the most from this chapter.

∗ The title of this book promises you'll learn how to experience joy, how to become a star, and how to have great hair days. In your journal, write out a short paragraph describing what you've learned about JOY. (Flip back to the following verses in Philippians if you need a quick refresher: 1:4; 1:25-26; 2:2; 2:29; 4:1.)

∗ How can you shine like a STAR? (Hike back to Philippians 2:15-16 if you need a hint.)

∗ Hopefully, you realize by now that having a great hair day has nothing to do with your hair. It has to do with what's happening on the inside. So, how can you have a great HAIR day? (Reread Philippians 4:11-13 and jot down how you can have a great hair day in spite of how your hair looks!)

∗ What stood out the most from the entire book of Philippians?

Do you hate looking at yourself in the mirror?

When you see your image, do you see everything that is wrong with you? Hair that doesn't look right or a body that you don't want? *Mirror, Mirror* is packed with raw honesty and truth, not easy answers or packaged solutions. It will help you think deeper about beauty, self-image, acceptance, health, sex, God's love, and more.

invert

RETAIL $12.99
ISBN 0310248868